Swift

by

J. MIDDLETON MURRY

Published for the British Council
by Longman Group Ltd

Forty New Pence net

In his succinct and penetrating survey of Swift's life and work, John Middleton Murry draws attention to the paradoxes that we everywhere encounter when we study that enigmatic figure. *Gulliver's Travels*, which has long been read as a fairy-tale by children, is in fact one of the most searing indictments of humanity ever penned; and its author deliberately shielded himself from all contact with children. Again, Swift, the apostle of rationalism, died with his splendid intellectual faculties in ruins; just as Swift, the Dean of St Patrick's, Dublin, and the champion of Ireland against English misgovernment, came to live in Ireland only because his hopes of power and preferment in England had been blasted. Middleton Murry shows how complex and baffling the contradictions in Swift's nature were, and how his comic genius barely managed to control them within the boundaries of his superb prose. And sometimes his savage indignation, his pathological disgust at humanity's folly and bestiality, shattered the perfection of his prose, revealing Swift's own tragic imagination.

Middleton Murry, who died in 1957, was one of the foremost literary critics of his day, the author of influential works on Keats and of a full-length biography of Swift. He is the subject of an essay by Philip Mairet in the present series.

¶ JONATHAN SWIFT was born in Dublin on 30 November 1667. He died there on 19 October 1745, and is buried in St Patrick's Cathedral.

SWIFT
from a painting by CHARLES JERVAS
National Portrait Gallery

SWIFT

by

J. MIDDLETON MURRY

PUBLISHED FOR
THE BRITISH COUNCIL
BY LONGMAN GROUP LTD

LONGMAN GROUP LTD
Longman House, Burnt Mill, Harlow, Essex

*Associated companies, branches and
representatives throughout the world*

*First published 1955
Reprinted 1961
Reprinted 1966, 1970 with additions to Bibliography*
© J. Middleton Murry 1961

*Printed in Great Britain by
F. Mildner & Sons, London, EC1*

SBN 0 582 01061 6

SWIFT

I

JONATHAN SWIFT is the most enigmatic and paradoxical figure among the great ones of English literature. Many have remarked on the irony by which *Gulliver's Travels*, in its entirety perhaps the most savage onslaught on humanity ever written, has come to be a classic of the nursery. Not so many have observed that this fate has befallen the greatest work of one who, at thirty-two, came to the solemn and strange resolve, which he seems to have kept religiously: 'Not to be fond of children, nor let them come near me hardly'. Or we may consider the mysterious dispensation by which the stubborn champion of rationality ended his life an imbecile; or the paradox by which the child-hater found release in the extraordinary convention by which he insisted on addressing Stella in his letters not as herself but as a compound of herself and her older companion, and addressing this composite in an embarrassing sort of baby language; or even the singular adventure of his early childhood, when he was stolen from his mother by a devoted nurse and kept apart from her till he was three. No matter where or how we lay hold of the story of Swift's life and work, we are baffled by mystery and mystification, by conflict and contradiction. We are acutely conscious, in his writing, of an immense power at work, yet deliberately channelled and applied under an equally great power of repression; on a few rare occasions working freely, for the most part confined to a particular task, and for long periods entirely suppressed. We have, moreover, to take seriously his confession to Pope:

All my endeavours from a boy to distinguish myself were only for want of a great title and fortune, that I might be used like a Lord by those who have an opinion of my parts—whether right or wrong it is no great matter, and so the reputation of wit or great learning does the office of a blue ribbon, or of a coach and six horses.

Undoubtedly, Swift used his genius as the instrument of his ambition; and his ambition was for power. Not for any kind of power—but for the power which literary genius, sternly disciplined to the particular purpose, might achieve for its possessor—the power of being feared and courted by the great ones of the earth. That was how he liked to regard himself:

> Grown old in politics and wit,
> Caress'd by ministers of state,
> Of half mankind the dread and hate.

It was no delusion of greatness. He had achieved the position he sought. And he had stripped himself for the arduous and difficult race. He sternly refused to become a professional author. Only once in his life did he ever receive pay for any original work: when the publisher paid £200 for Gulliver, a fantastically small amount compared with what Pope—or even Prior—made out of a book. Only once in his life did he put his own name to a piece of his writing: *A Proposal for Correcting, Improving and Ascertaining the English Tongue*. The motives behind this sedulous anonymity were complex; but perhaps the chief was to maintain an aura of mystery and to give himself the maximum possibility of manœuvre. And behind it all was a fierce pride, which could never bear to fail. Let that only be his, which could be nobody else's.

For the race he also stripped himself of the encumbrance of marriage. Volumes have been written, and will be written, concerning his relations with the two women who loved him, and indeed gave up their lives to loving him: Stella (Esther Johnson) and Vanessa (Esther Vanhomrigh). For the moment it is sufficient to say that, although he particularly enjoyed and was dependent upon the society of women, he deliberately renounced marriage as an impediment when he determined to make his career.

Twice he reached the pinnacle of his ambition, in two vastly different scenes. First, in 1710-13, when he became the incomparable literary champion of Harley's Tory ministry: when he potently assailed the Duke of Marlborough and defended the Treaty of Utrecht. No more consummate political journalism has ever been written than Swift's *Examiners*. The price he exacted for his services was to be admitted to the personal friendship of Harley and St John. Without that, they would never have got him, or certainly never have kept him.

He reached at it again, under adverse conditions, when he had been 'banished' to the deanery of St Patrick's, and the Tories had fallen at the death of Queen Anne. Then, after a long period of silence, he emerged as the champion of Irish economic independence and subsequently as the inspiriter of the nation-wide agitation against Wood's Halfpence. Almost in spite of himself, for he was an impassioned defender of the privileges of the Church of Ireland, he became the national hero of Protestants and Papists alike: the first of the kind. The 'Drapier's Letters' kindled a spark of Irish patriotism which did not cease to glow for two hundred years.

These were astonishing practical achievements for the written word. What was behind them? Of what kind was the fund of genius of which this unique journalism was the narrowed application? First and foremost, a comic power of unparalleled intensity and alarming scope. On the rare occasions when Swift gave unfettered utterance, it appears as formidable and terrifying. Nothing seems sacred from its fierce power of destruction. When, as in *A Tale of a Tub*, he professed, perhaps sincerely, to use it in defence of the Church of England against the aberrations of Papism on the one side and Dissent on the other, his conscious purposes are nullified by the poetic fury of his universal irreverence. The authorities of the Church he professed to champion were horrified by his methods, which he himself afterwards aptly symbolized when Captain Lemuel Gulliver puts out the fire in the Empress's palace by pissing on it. In *Gulliver's Travels* itself its comic power ceases to be light-hearted. Humanity in his eyes is long past being a joke. The embers of the wild fun of *A Tale of a Tub* are quenched in the fierce indignation which, as his chosen epitaph says, tore at his heart.

To attempt to analyse the causes of this comic intensity is vain. One must accept as a datum the demonic power of Swift's genius. But it is interesting to observe that it did not declare itself until he was thirty years of age. All that he wrote, or all that has survived of his writing, before 1697 is laborious, but curiously personal, attempts at Pindaric poetry in the manner of Cowley, quite unlike any of his later work in verse or prose. In these he reveals himself as one seeking poetic inspiration in his admiration for the great and good, though struggling with a strong impulse to attack the evil that threatened them. They end abruptly with a remarkable confession at once of thwarted affection and poetic failure, and conclude with a passionate denunciation of the ideal—and the poetic inspiration given by the ideal—as illusion:

> And from this hour
> I here renounce thy visionary power;
> And since thy essence on my breath depends,
> Thus, with a puff, the whole delusion ends.

The poem is the most naked piece of self-revelation in all Swift's writings. It plainly shows that some sort of psychological crisis preceded the manifestation of his formidable genius in the form we know. And it shows that one great factor in the crisis was his intense chagrin at not having achieved a secure place in the affections of Sir William Temple. It is worth bearing in mind that the Swift we know, the marks of whose suppressed passionate nature are so unmistakable, was at a critical moment an emotionally frustrated man.

II

He was born in Dublin in 1667, the son of a young lawyer who, with older brothers of his English family, mainly of the same profession, had gone to Ireland after the Restoration to seek their fortunes. His father had not had time to begin making his when he died, at the age of twenty-seven, before Swift was born. His mother was left with a bare £20 a year. Swift started life as a poor relation. He was educated at an uncle's expense at Kilkenny College and Trinity, where he was humiliated by his poverty and resentful of the curriculum. He just scraped his degree. At some period, probably when he was sent to Kilkenny, at six years old, his mother returned to her home near Leicester. So that we must imagine Swift, from six to twenty-two, existing without father or mother, on the rather grudging charity of relations—while submitting to 'the education of a dog', as he called it bitterly.

In 1689, during the Irish 'troubles', he was taken into Sir William Temple's house at Moor Park as secretary, where he made friends with the little girl Esther Johnson (Stella), a daughter of the waiting-woman of Temple's sister, Lady Giffard. Stella was a favourite of the house, and had been virtually adopted by Temple. After the battle of the Boyne, Swift returned to Ireland in the hope of picking up a job with Temple's recommendation, He failed and returned to Moor Park, where he stayed, reading hard and widely, writing poetry, and acting as secretary, till May 1694 (the time of crisis to which we have referred), when he picked a quarrel with Temple and left abruptly to seek a career in the Church of Ireland. Temple behaved generously, and gave him the testimonial necessary to his ordination. In January 1695, Swift entered on a modest living near Carrickfergus. There he fell in love with a Miss Jane Waring (Varina) and pressed her hard to marry him. She hesitated, and refused his ultimatum—a remarkable letter which has survived. Swift then shook the dust of Ireland off his feet and returned in April 1696, at Temple's pressing invitation, to Moor Park. Varina's rejection of him was perhaps decisive in Swift's renunciation of marriage.

He now stayed with Temple until his sudden death in

January 1699, when he was left his literary executor. During the final three years at Moor Park Stella was a young woman. She fell in love, permanently, with Swift, while he allowed himself to entertain, also permanently, a platonic affection for her. During this time he wrote the volume called *A Tale of a Tub*, though it was not published till 1704.

Since this book had a direct effect on his subsequent career, it must be described briefly here. The most attractive part of it for the reader who has not acquired a taste for the wilder, grimmer Swift is *The Battle of the Books*. In origin this is a gay intervention in the excited dispute which had arisen out of an essay by Temple on *Ancient and Modern Learning*, in which he had deprecated the pride of the moderns in their scientific achievements. These had, he said, diverted philosophy from its more important concern, with ethics, wherein the ancients still far excelled them. In effect Temple's essay was a cogent criticism of the nascent dogma of automatic progress. But Temple was not an exact scholar—he regarded the Epistles of Phalaris as of high antiquity and praised them extravagantly—and he was unduly contemptuous of the scientific movement, of which he knew nothing. A young FRS, the Revd William Wotton, made a careful and polite reply to the latter strictures, and the famous Bentley, in an appendix to Wotton's book, rather roughly but finally demolished the authenticity of Phalaris.

Swift, sympathetic to Temple and his argument, enjoyed himself poking fun at Bentley and Wotton in a burlesque of Homer, describing a fight between the ancient and modern volumes in St James's Library. It was not a serious contribution to the controversy. Dryden, who had told Swift that he would never make a Pindaric poet, is ridiculed just as mercilessly as Temple's critics. But it was a brilliant preliminary canter of his comic Pegasus, and it sparkles still.

The rest of the book was heavier metal. *The Mechanical Operation of the Spirit* is an extravaganza on the theme that the inspiration of the Nonconformists is sexual in origin. In the *Tale* itself, though the Dissenters are still a target, the book becomes a wild discourse on the folly of inspiration of every kind, including its own. It starts from a ribald parable of the history of the Christian Church, in which Peter, Martin and Jack—all disreputable characters—represent the Roman, the Anglican and the Dissenting Churches respectively; but it wanders off into a maze of Digressions. It is a close-knit sequence of ostensibly rational nonsense. Satire, in any accepted sense of the word, it is not. Swift, behind the alias of an ex-Bedlamite Grub Street author, reduces the world to an absurd chaos of relativity: all idealisms are madness, all sciences futile, all philosophies hallucination; the best is 'the serene peaceful state of being a fool among knaves'. Subsequently he claimed that it was a defence of the Church of England, and perhaps he may have begun it with such a purpose; but an irrepressible and irresponsible comic invention snatched it out of the hands of Swift the clergyman. The genius of the book is indubitable; the difficulty is to conceive with what conception of religion or his priestly function Swift believed it congruous. He allowed the harmless *Battle of the Books* to circulate in manuscript, and put the rest away.

After Temple's death, Swift waited about the Court for some months in the hope of securing an English prebend, which Temple (he said) had promised to obtain for him. He waited in vain, and reluctantly—for he did not want to return to Ireland—accepted the best offer available: an appointment as chaplain-secretary to Lord Berkeley, one of the new Irish Lords Justices. On his arrival in Dublin he was given the living of Laracor and, shortly after, a prebend in St Patrick's. Swift, as usual, thought he deserved better; but he had now an income of £250 a year—useful enough in those days.

He was thirty-three. Though he was by no means reconciled to a future in Ireland, he took the important step of persuading Stella to make her home in Dublin. She had as her duenna Rebecca Dingley—a kinswoman of Temple, who lived with her at Moor Park. He paid 'the ladies', as he called them, an allowance of £50 a year. This, with Temple's substantial legacy to Stella of £1,500, enabled them to live modestly as gentlewomen. In the same year, 1701, he made his entry into English political writing by publishing a well-argued *Discourse of the Contests and Dissensions between the Nobles and the Commons in Athens and Rome*. This was a sound exposition of the essentials of the British constitution and a cogent demonstration of the dangers of the process of impeachment, with which the Tories were threatening the Whig statesmen who had endorsed King William's foreign policy. It brought him to the familiar acquaintance of Somers and Halifax and, in their entourage, of the Whig wits, Addison and Steele. Congreve he had known at Trinity; Prior also was his friend.

By virtue of his pamphlet, and his political acquaintance, Swift now had the reputation of being a moderate Whig. Actually, he had not thought out his political position; and, in fact, he was just as near to being a moderate Tory. He was definitely opposed to the sentimental Jacobitism of the high-flying Tories; he was also opposed to diminishing (or increasing) the political disabilities of the Dissenters. But in a general way he was ready to lend a helping hand to any of the moderate politicians who would be likely to reward him with an English preferment. Whether he actually wrote anything more for the Whigs is unknown—except a pamphlet against the high Tory attack on Occasional Conformity which he wrote in 1704. But it came too late, and he destroyed it.

Why he chose this moment to publish *A Tale of a Tub* is obscure; but it may be connected with the fact that publication was followed by his longest continuous stay in Ireland since he left Trinity—nearly three and a half years. That suggests that for the time being he had renounced his pursuit of a career in England. That he did this on political grounds is very improbable, for the Godolphin ministry was taking on an increasingly Whig complexion. More likely he retired to Ireland because Stella had come near to letting herself be married to a friend of his. Swift realized that if he wanted to keep her he must stay near her. If he had temporarily resigned his English hopes, it was a good moment for publishing the *Tale*, which, while it was bound vastly to increase his literary reputation, was also bound to be an obstacle to his preferment. It was a huge success; and Swift wittily improved it by incorporating many of the criticisms of the Revd W. Wotton as solemn explanatory notes.

During his stay in Ireland Swift wrote practically nothing except the charming humorous poem, 'Baucis and Philemon'. He seems to have given himself up to enjoying life in the company of Stella in Dublin and at Laracor, and to improving his standing in the Church of Ireland. When he eventually returned to England, in November 1707, it was as the official emissary of that Church, charged with obtaining the support of the politicians for the extension of Queen Anne's Bounty to Ireland. The 'ladies' went to London at the same time; but the attractions of the centre of power were too much for him, and he abandoned his plan of returning with them. Moreover, the Whigs now dominated the ministry, and his hopes were raised accordingly. Nothing came of them. He allowed himself to be put forward by Somers for the post of chaplain to Wharton, the new Lord Lieutenant—a post which was regarded as the shortest way to an Irish bishopric—but he was passed over because of his opposition to the removal of the Test Act in Ireland.

To this return to England belongs some of his most brilliant comic writing: the glorious sustained joke of Isaac Bickerstaff Esq.'s *Predictions for the Year 1708*, foretelling the death of Partridge the almanac-maker, and the dazzling *Argument against Abolishing Christianity*. He also put out some more sober political pamphlets, in which he sought to define his own position, and argued for the formation of a Court party of the centre, which should unite the moderate Tories and the moderate Whigs. He also prepared a new edition of *A Tale of a Tub*, prefixing an Apology which shows him well aware of the harm it had done him with the Queen's ecclesiastical adviser, the Archbishop of York. Perhaps he tried to rehabilitate himself by his *Project for the Advancement of Religion*, which was an appeal to the Queen to insist on a decent moral character as a qualification for office. But at the same time he made a bad mistake, by defying the wishes of the Temple family in publishing the third part of Sir William Temple's *Memoirs*, in which the writer severely condemns the character of Lord Essex, who was involved in Shaftesbury's plot and committed suicide in the Tower. Lady Essex, his widow, was the favourite aunt of the Duchess of Somerset, who was outraged by Swift's indefensible behaviour, and wrote to Temple's sister:

> It was not proper to be made public during my Aunt Essex's life, and I am sure Dr Swift has too much wit to think it is, which makes his having done it unpardonable and will confirm me in the opinion I had before of him that he is a man of no principle either of honour, or of religion.

Eighteen months later the Duchess of Marlborough was dismissed, and the Duchess of Somerset succeeded her as the Queen's most intimate servant. Her opinion of Swift was to prove fatal to his hopes of preferment in England.

Before Swift returned to Ireland in June 1709, Steele, with his full approval, had seized the opportunity of the popularity Swift had won in the name of Isaac Bickerstaff to launch *The Tatler* as the vehicle for his lucubrations. Though Swift himself did not contribute much to it, beyond two admirable humorous poems on London life, 'A Description of the Morning' and 'A City Shower', he supplied Steele with a fund of ideas—'hints' as he called them—which were an important factor in the prodigious success of that epoch-making periodical.

He now spent over a year in Ireland, much of it in the company of Addison who was there as Wharton's secretary. Addison appreciated Stella; and that, perhaps as much as the genuine mutual admiration of the two men of genius, kept them friends when their political paths sharply diverged. But at this time Swift still regarded himself as a sort of Whig, and on the major political issue of the time— war or peace with France—he was one. He was, rather unthinkingly, for Marlborough and the war. So that when the news came of the imminent downfall of the Whig ministry, he was perplexed what to do. However, his hesitation was decided by a fresh commission by the Irish Church to make contact with the new Tory government, and press its claim to Queen Anne's Bounty. He left Dublin on 31 August 1710 and did not return till June 1713, when he returned as Dean of St Patrick's.

The detailed story of this fascinating period of his life is told in the *Journal to Stella*, to which there is nothing comparable in our literature. Within a few weeks of his arrival Swift was on intimate terms with Harley; he had taken over *The Examiner* and become the chief literary champion of the new ministry. Harley laid himself out, as none of the Whig grandees had ever done, to win Swift over. He instantly granted the request of the Irish Church, instructed him as to the necessity of peace, informed him of Marlborough's unwarrantable rejection of the French overtures, and promised him, in reward for his assistance in advocating peace, discrediting Marlborough, and discomfiting the Whigs, the best preferment he could obtain for him. It is probable that Harley himself was unaware of all the obstacles in the way, for there is no reason to suppose he knew of the offence Swift had given to the Duchess of Somerset. But, reading between the lines of the *Journal*, it is plain that after the Duchess of Somerset had taken the Duchess of Marlborough's place, there was no possibility of Swift's entering into favour with the Queen.

Swift is often charged with having turned his coat politically. There is no substance in the charge. Harley's moderate Toryism was indistinguishable from Swift's moderate Whiggism; and Harley's attitude to the Church was far more congenial to Swift than that of the Whigs. On the

matter of war and peace there is no evidence that he had
really thought at all until he came under the influence of
Harley and St John; and it was no disgrace to him that they
converted him, for they were in the right.

Swift's work on *The Examiner* was convinced and brilliant. It lasted from November 1710 to June 1711, when he
dropped it to write *The Conduct of the Allies*. That pamphlet,
justly famous though it is, suffers by comparison with the
best of the *Examiners*. One feels that Swift was too oppressed
by his task to indulge his mordant wit. A more characteristic
effort of his was *A New Journey to Paris*, which professed
to be an account by Prior's French courier of his doings in
Paris, whither he had been sent on a secret mission to nego-
tiate the preliminaries of the Treaty of Utrecht. By a mis-
understanding, Prior was arrested at Dover, and the secret
mission became known: a contretemps which might have
been highly embarrassing to the ministry. Swift promptly
turned it to good account. The fictitious narrative was
plausible enough to impose upon everybody, and it repre-
sented Prior as taking a very high hand indeed with
Louis XIV. It is a remarkable example of the quick origin-
ality of Swift's mind, and of the talent for mystification
in which he delighted.

During the political crisis which followed the virtual
rejection of the Treaty by the Lords on 7 December 1711,
Swift lost his nerve. He was convinced that the government
must fall, and was afraid for himself. Because the Duke of
Somerset, who formerly supported Harley, was now
intriguing against him, Swift persuaded himself that the
Duchess of Somerset was in the plot, and that the only
salvation for the government lay in forcing the Queen to
dismiss her. To this end he wrote a vicious lampoon against
her, *The Windsor Prophecy*. It was quite unforgivable. Unless
the Duchess were dismissed, he had absolutely ruined his
chance of promotion in the English Church. The crisis was
boldly overcome by Harley: Marlborough was dismissed,
Somerset was dismissed but the Duchess remained.

Swift wanted an English deanery. He gave Harley to understand that when the first suitable preferment was given away from him he would return forthwith to Ireland. Harley seems to have done his best; but the Queen was adamant. The utmost that could be contrived for him was the Deanery of St Patrick's. That was finally settled on 23 April 1713, at the end of a period of suspense which had lasted over a year. During most of it Swift was desultorily occupied with a historical narrative of the making of the Treaty of Utrecht. But by that time the tension between Harley and St John had grown so great that Swift felt his narrative was bound to offend one or the other, and he suspended work. The cleavage between the great men increased his nervousness concerning the future. He sought relief from his anxiety in the society of Vanessa who, by the time he went to Dublin to be installed as Dean, had fallen passionately in love with him. She was then twenty-five: seven years younger than Stella. At this time he wrote, evidently for Vanessa's private enjoyment, the long poem 'Cadenus and Vanessa', which describes the process of their emotional entanglement, and concludes with a famous and characteristic ambiguity:

> But what success Vanessa met
> Is to the world a secret yet.
> Whether the nymph to please her swain,
> Talks in a high romantic strain;
> Or whether he at last descends
> To like with less seraphic ends;
> Or to compound the business, whether
> They temper love and books together,
> Must never to mankind be told,
> Nor shall the conscious Muse unfold.

After four months in Ireland, during which he was mostly depressed and ill, Swift returned to London. The quarrel between the ministers had now become a bitter feud, and St John was intriguing hard to take Harley's place. Swift was quite impotent to heal the breach between them, which was one of high policy as well as personal ambition. There is no evidence that Swift really understood either the issues at stake or St John's manœuvres. He wrote some trenchant and witty pamphlets, but they were mainly in prosecution of a quarrel with Steele, who had become a violent Whig politician. Of his alarmist pamphlet, *The Crisis*, Swift made merciless fun. But the divided ministry had no line to give him. The death of the Queen, the accession of the Hanoverian, and the downfall of the Tories was now certain. Nothing could avert the animus of the new King against the architects of the Treaty of Utrecht.

On 31 May 1714 Swift went into retirement at Letcombe in Berkshire. He wrote a pamphlet, *Some Free Thoughts on the Present State of Affairs*, which the printer submitted to St John, and St John suppressed. When Harley was finally dismissed, on 27 July, Swift refused to support St John. He waited a fortnight after the death of the Queen to see what would happen; then slipped away to Dublin to take the oaths and resume his Deanery. He was now forty-seven. His connection with English politics was ended.

For the next six years, Swift took no part in Irish politics either. He was suspected to be a Jacobite. So he lay *perdu* and devoted himself to the organization of his Deanery, and the better ordering of the Cathedral; also to the delicate business of reconciling the claims upon himself of Stella and Vanessa, who had followed him to Ireland. On the whole the weight of the evidence on this obscure and debatable subject is that, in order to reassure Stella, he was secretly married to her in 1716. It was a purely nominal marriage, which in no way prevented him from acknowledging Vanessa's claim on his affection. But that unhappy woman's passion demanded more than he could give. She was tubercular and emotionally tormented. When, in 1723, she learned that Swift was married to Stella, her thin flame of life soon flickered out.

Meanwhile, having lived down the unwarrantable suspicion of Jacobitism, Swift had resumed his natural place as a champion of the Irish interest. Under Walpole and the Whigs the exploitation of Ireland had become more systematic. In 1720 Swift, outraged by an Act of the English Parliament entirely subordinating the Irish to the English legislature, tried to inspirit a boycott of English manufacturers by a pamphlet which ends with a scathing denunciation of the Irish landlords:

I have heard great divines affirm that 'nothing is so likely to call down an universal judgment from Heaven upon a nation as universal oppression'; and whether this be not already verified in part, their worships the landlords are now at full leisure to consider. Whoever travels this country, and observes the face of nature, or the faces, and habits, and dwellings of the natives, will hardly think himself in a land where either law, religion, or common humanity is professed.

Almost in spite of himself, and probably without ever fully admitting it to consciousness, Swift was becoming the champion of Papists as well as Protestants.

His attitude demands a word of explanation. Swift remained quite unbending in his defence of the supremacy of the Church of Ireland; he was always implacably opposed to admitting even Irish Presbyterians to political rights. But he was a passionate champion of Irish economic independence. Further, he was in favour of giving the native Irish a chance to live by restraining the landlords from ruthlessly converting pasture to tillage. In this, it is true, the interests of the Church of Ireland, which depended on its tithe, coincided with those of the peasants. But there is no reason to doubt that Swift was, at least in part, disinterested in his indignation at the miserable condition of the native Irish.

On both counts the authorities took alarm at his pamphlet, and the printer was vindictively prosecuted. There was no practical outcome to Swift's appeal for a boycott of English manufacturers. He drew in his horns again, and applied himself to the writing of *Gulliver's Travels*.

Probably his absorption in that work accounts for the

fact that he did not participate in the agitation against Wood's Halfpence until it had already reached a considerable height. Wood's iniquitous patent, which had been obtained by a bribe of £10,000 to George I's German mistress, the Duchess of Kendal, and which would have enabled him to make a profit of £40,000 on supplying Ireland with a new copper coinage, had been granted on 12 July 1722. The Irish Commons acted with unusual resolution, and presented strong addresses to the King against it, and a widespread movement of resistance had begun before Swift intervened with the first of the 'Drapier's Letters' in February 1724: *A Letter to the Shop-Keepers, Tradesmen, Farmers and Common People of Ireland*. It is a masterpiece of popular writing, in a sense unscrupulous in its exaggerations and demagoguery, but with a characteristic streak of wild humour, driving home his two main points: that the new coinage will mean ruin to the common man, if he accepts it, and that the King himself has not the power to compel him to do so. It ran like wildfire. A second 'Letter' followed in August, in which the Drapier called for a boycott of any tradesmen who attempted to pass the coins; a third, three weeks later, was a careful reply to the favourable report of the English Privy Council on the Patent, and was primarily addressed to the Irish Parliament to prevent its being intimidated by the Report. The fourth, *A Letter to the Whole People of Ireland*, published just in time to greet the arrival of the new Lord Lieutenant, Carteret, in October, was a direct challenge to English supremacy. It is a contemptuous repudiation of the King's prerogative, and a stirring appeal to the common man to be master of his own national destiny. Let him not bother his head with rumours that English authority will enforce or withdraw the Patent:

The remedy is wholly in your hands, and therefore I have digressed a little in order to refresh and continue the spirit so seasonably raised among you, and to let you see that by the laws of GOD, of NATURE, of NATIONS and of your own COUNTRY, you ARE and OUGHT to be as FREE people as your brethren in England.

That was a direct repudiation of the English Act of 1720. A proclamation was immediately issued againt the printer. Swift then wrote a brilliant *Letter to the Lord Chancellor*, which however he suppressed. Had it appeared it would have had the effect of making him appear in person as the leader of the agitation, though not as the author of the 'Drapier's Letters'. He would have, so to speak, taken over the lead from the Drapier. But he, wisely, decided not to do so, and applied himself to inspiriting the jury to reject the charge against the printer. It did that, and more; it indicted 'all such persons as have attempted, or shall endeavour, to impose the said Halfpence upon us'.

Carteret, by now, was pressing the home government to withdraw the Patent. While it was demurring the Drapier wrote two more 'Letters', of which the last was an appeal to the Irish Commons to assume the moral leadership of 'the whole people of Ireland', and to the people to obey its votes, whether they received the Royal Assent or not. In short, Ireland was to act as an independent nation. Before *The Humble Address* could appear, the Patent was withdrawn on 19 August 1725, and Swift suppressed his pamphlet. He realized that his aim to enlarge and uplift the agitation against the Halfpence into a nation-wide movement of non-co-operation with England was chimerical. Probably, from the beginning he had been under no illusion; but he could not resist the opportunity of trying his power.

Stella was now in a decline. Chiefly to avoid the torment of watching her die, Swift paid long visits to England in 1726 and 1727 and became loosely attached to the 'opposition' court of the Prince and Princess of Wales. He entertained a faint hope of an English preferment when, as he believed, Walpole would be dislodged, at the death of George I. Probably, his desire was to leave Ireland which, with Stella gone, would be a land of ghosts for him. But, though the King died, Walpole became stronger than before. Swift returned reluctantly to Dublin to face the ordeal of Stella's final illness. She died on 28 January 1728.

There is a circumstantial story that she requested to be acknowledged as his wife, and that he refused. If the story is true, he did right to refuse. Such acknowledgement would have given a totally false impression of their relation.

His sense of isolation now became extreme; but he kept a grip upon himself. He wrote more Irish political pamphlets, culminating in the most famous of all, *A Modest Proposal* that one hundred thousand native Irish children should be fattened for market at a year old: a masterpiece of macabre humour, written from a fund of despair. By violent exercise he fought stubbornly against his own increasing deafness and giddiness, caused by a disease of the labyrinth of the ear. His personal economy became obsessive: he was saving to endow a lunatic asylum. A national hero, already almost a national legend, he stalked about the liberty of St Patrick's, doing endless small charities with a grim face. Complete control of himself became a greater effort, both in personal behaviour and in writing. Not only did he explode into scatalogical verse, in which his abhorrence of the human animal is pathologically vehement, but such excellent poetry as 'The Death of Dr Swift' and 'The Life and Character of Dr Swift' is partly spoiled by the outbursts of irrelevant passion. Once, however, in 'The Legion Club', a scathing onslaught on the Irish Commons, passion itself was inspiration. This scalding invective has good claim to be considered Swift's finest poem. It was written in 1735, the occasion being an attack by the Irish Commons on the revenues of the Church of Ireland.

He amused himself with incredibly complicated exercises in a sort of dog-Latin; and, more seriously, with slowly elaborating Simon Wagstaff's *Complete Collection of Genteel and Ingenious Conversation*—an unsparing record of conversational inanity which freezes the smile on the reader's face —and the never finished *Directions to Servants*, which have plenty of the old wild humour to keep them fresh. He also supervised, while ostensibly disowning, the beautiful collected edition of his works published by Faulkner in Dublin.

It did not include *A Tale of a Tub*, for reasons which must be conjectured.

Swift became more and more of a recluse, and more and more capricious and irritable in his behaviour to his friends. He was subject to lapses of memory, and entertained fantasies about his own past. Long periods of profound lethargy, probably due to sheer physical exhaustion, seized him. From 1738 he was hardly responsible for his own actions, for his periods of entire lucidity were intermittent. In one of them he made his will, on 4 May 1740, with some characteristic jokes. But he was practically unapproachable. In August 1742 his friends requested a commission of lunacy upon him. His mind seems finally to have failed in the previous May. In October he endured great physical agony; but afterwards he sank into a condition of imbecility, which lasted three years. He died on 19 October 1745. Above his grave in St Patrick's was set the Latin epitaph he had commanded in his will. The English runs:

The body of Jonathan Swift, Doctor of Divinity, Dean of this Cathedral, is buried here, where fierce indignation can tear at his heart no more. Go, traveller, and imitate if you can one who strove his utmost to champion human liberty.

III

The personal history of Swift cannot be avoided. We know far more about him than we do about many of his contemporaries, we feel him as a man far more: Defoe, Addison, Congreve, even Pope, are shadowy figures compared to him. It is not merely that they have left no documents comparable to the *Journal to Stella;* or that he was a man of affairs as well as a man of letters—so, even more, was Addison. We feel that it is somehow the consequence of his having been a much more dynamic personality than writers—even the very greatest—are wont to be. Thackeray's famous verdict: 'So great a man he seems to me, that thinking of him is like thinking of an empire falling' corresponds to our sense and sentiment.

To attempt, therefore, to judge him by his pure literary achievement, or even to judge his writings themselves as things that exist *per se*, seems always faintly irrelevant. One is continually conscious in them of a deliberate self-repression, and of an immense energy applied to the task of holding himself in leash. Whereas with a Shakespeare, a Chaucer or even a Dickens or a Conrad, we feel that their works do completely reveal them, with Swift our abiding impression is that the essential personality of the man is somewhat outside his work—lurking, at best, inscrutibly on the edge of them. It is so with the greatest of them. *Where* is the author of *A Tale of a Tub*? *Where* is the author of *Gulliver*?

Swift is forever assuming a mask: not only formally as in that large portion of his work which puports to be written by some fictitious character—the Bedlamite, Bicker-staff, Du Baudrier, Captain Gulliver, the Drapier—but he constantly writes from somewhere off centre. In relatively few of his writings can we say with any confidence: *ipse dixit*. Such concealment, it is true, is to some degree technical; it can be explained as a mechanism to facilitate the exaggerations, the distortions, the multiplicity of slants, which are congenial, and probably essential, to the comic vision, and as having its prototype in the poker face (deliberately cultivated by Swift) which proffers some wild enormity as sober fact.

But in Swift it is more than this. One senses an underlying and less variable *persona* as a necessity of tolerable existence: a deliberately adopted means of escape from an emotional nature that threatened to overwhelm him. Tender, generous, passionate, and perhaps also *malade de l'idéal*—these elements were to him so many sources of weakness that had to be stopped at all costs in one who would battle with the world. The picture of him left by Vanessa:

> Sometimes you strike me with that prodigious awe, I tremble with fear; at other times a charming compassion shines through your countenance which revives my soul.

is convincing to one well read in his works. He stood inces-
santly on guard against his affections and emotions which
menaced the citadel of his rationality and would sweep him
from the rock of his self-control. He suffered his tenderness
to play chiefly in the form of protectiveness towards those
less well armoured than himself. He was responsive to
integrity, revolted by injustice, and outraged by what he felt
to be the basic irrationality of human existence. Of its
animal substrate he came to feel a morbid horror.

Swift's reputation among his friends was that of 'a man
of mirth'. To Fielding, who was no bad judge, he was 'the
greatest master of humour that ever wrote'. Those contemporary verdicts have been overshadowed by a later sense of
the gloom and savagery that invaded his writing. The
emphasis has shifted, and the picture has been unduly
darkened. It is not so much that the truth lies between, as
that Swift's comic genius worked on two levels of intensity
which are manifest, at the outset, in the contrast, between
A Tale of a Tub and *The Battle of the Books*. On the one level
is a universal derision and a ruthless exposure of the human
condition, an attitude in which there is acceptance of
nothing; on the other level there is a pragmatic acceptance of
the necessity of passing life within the common forms, of
averting one's eyes from the abyss, or the heights for that
matter, and being a reasonable man. At this level his humour
is genial and sometimes beautifully urbane. And, speaking
roughly, it is on this level that his genius mainly functioned
in the long interval between his two major works, *A Tale
of a Tub* (1697) and *Gulliver* (1721-5). There is an astonish-
ingly rich variety in his minor works during the early part
of this period. In verse alone, 'Mrs Francis Harris's Petition',
'Baucis and Philemon', 'A Description of the Morning', and
'A City Shower' each open a new vein. In prose there is
Isaac Bickerstaff's Predictions and the *Argument against Abolishing Christianity*, and the innumerable diverting divagations
of his more serious pamphlets. Though some of the savour
of his more audacious jokes is dulled by time, anyone who

cares to steep himself in the exciting political history of Queen Anne's reign will find they live again. And all the while he was perfecting the instrument of his superb polemical prose.

This is markedly different from the prose of *A Tale of a Tub*, in which he gave full rein to the first great flight of his comic Pegasus. That has an unbridled opulence of invention, which he afterwards eschewed, perhaps thinking it too dangerous to his prospects to be indulged. Because of the many varieties of manner it is not easy to choose a characteristic specimen from this 'wild work', as Dr Johnson called it; but perhaps the two following, both with hints of personal experience, may indicate something of the range of style and thought:

And whereas the mind of a man, when he gives the spur and bridle to his thoughts, doth never stop, but naturally sallies out into both extremes, of high and low, of good and evil, his first flight of fancy commonly transports him to ideas of what is most perfect, finished, and exhalted; till, having soared out of his own reach and sight, not well perceiving how near the frontiers of height and depth border upon each other; with the same course and wing, he falls down plumb into the lowest bottom of things, like one who travels the east into the west, or like a straight line drawn by its own length, into a circle. Whether a tincture of malice in our natures makes us fond of furnishing every bright idea with its reverse; or whether reason, reflecting on the sum of things, can, like the sun, serve only to enlighten one half of the globe, leaving the other half by necessity under shade and darkness; or, whether fancy, flying up to the imagination of what is highest and best, becomes overshot, and spent, and weary, and suddenly falls, like a dead bird of paradise, to the ground; or whether, after all these metaphysical conjectures, I have not entirely missed the true reason; the proposition, however, which has stood me in so much circumstance, is altogether true; that, as the most uncivilized parts of mankind have some way or other climbed up to the conception of a God, so they have seldom forgot to provide their fears with ghastly notions, which, instead of better, have served them pretty tolerably for a devil.

That is from the excursus on Æolism, or the doctrine of inspiration by wind. The following is from one of the

Bedlamite author's frequent eulogies of his own 'divine treatise':

> Now it is not well enough considered, to what accidents and occasions the world is indebted for the greatest part of those noble writings, which hourly start up to entertain it. If it were not for a rainy day, a drunken vigil, a fit of the spleen, a course of physic, a sleepy Sunday, an ill run at dice, a long tailor's bill, a beggar's purse, a factious head, a hot sun, costive diet, want of books, and a just contempt of learning—out of these events, I say, and some others too long to recite (especially a prudent neglect of taking brimstone inwardly) I doubt, the number of authors and of writings would dwindle away to a degree most woful to behold. To confirm this opinion, hear the words of the famous Troglodyte philosopher: ''Tis certain', (said he) 'some grains of folly are of course annexed as part of the composition of human nature, only the choice is left to us, whether we please to wear them inlaid or embossed, and we need not go very far to seek how that is usually determined, when we remember it is with human faculties as with liquors, the lightest will ever be on top.'

The Troglodyte philosopher is Swift himself, and the ironic reference is to a sandy cave in the grounds of Moor Park in which he used to seek the poetic inspiration of which he is now derisive.

This in a dozen years becomes the much more sternly controlled prose of *The Examiner*, which is like a perfectly reasonable, perfectly modulated conversation, with always a smiling hint of strength in reserve. The opening page of his first *Examiner* is entirely characteristic:

> It is a practice I have generally followed, to converse with equal freedom with the deserving men of both parties; and it was never without some contempt, that I have observed persons wholly out of employment [i.e. without government office], affect to do otherwise: I doubted whether any man could owe so much to the side he was of, though he were retained by it; but without some great point of interest, either in possession or prospect, I thought it was the mark of a low and narrow spirit.

> It is hard that for some weeks past, I have been forced, in my own defence, to follow a proceeding that I have so much condemned in

others. But several of my acquaintance, among the declining party, are grown so insufferably peevish and splenetic, profess such violent apprehesions for the public [i.e. the *res publica*], and represent the state of things in such formidable ideas, that I find myself disposed to share in their afflictions, although I know them to be groundless and imaginary, or, which is worse, purely affected. To offer them comfort one by one would not only be an endless, but a disobliging task. Some of them, I am convinced, would be less melancholy, if there were more occasion. I shall therefore, instead of hearkening to further complaints, employ some part of this paper for the future, in letting such men see, that their natural or acquired fears are ill-grounded, and their artificial ones as ill-intended.

The economy and vigour of this prose is perfect, the just-submerged humour delightful; and how suavely deceptive is the sudden thrust he gives the alarmist Whigs in 'Some of them, I am convinced, would be less melancholy, if there were more occasion'! To think that writing of this quality had a positive political effect is to realize how transitory were the conditions under which Swift became a power in English politics. Certainly the 'Drapier's Letters' show that he could have adapted himself to conditions more analagous to those of a democracy; but, remarkable as they are, they have not the sustained perfection of the *Examiners*, or of Swift's political writings as a whole from 1708 to the death of the Queen.

But Swift found the imposed restraint irksome. There is evidence in the *Journal* that he put more sheer hard work than is generally supposed into his writings championing the Tories and harrying the Whigs. It was not easy writing for him. And one feels that he had been more at his ease when he still felt free to blow both parties sky-high, as in the *Argument against Abolishing Christianity*. Fully to appreciate this, one must come to it with a fresh memory of the incessant Tory motion in Parliament that 'the Church is in danger'. Then the gorgeous joke of the following, 'among the inconveniences that may be caused' by the abolition of Christianity, appears in its true magnificence:

Nor do I think it wholly groundless, or my fears altogether imaginary, that the abolishing of Christianity may perhaps bring the Church into danger, or at least put the Senate to the trouble of another securing vote. I desire I may not be mistaken; I am far from presuming to affirm or to think that the Church is in danger at present, or as things now stand, but we know not how soon it may be so when the Christian religion is repealed . . . Therefore, this may be intended as one political step toward altering the constitution of the Church established.

That is the irreverent comic fantasy in its sublime. The vision Swift conjures up of the Whig majority, having repealed the Christian religion solemnly voting that the Church is *not* in danger; and the spectacle of the High Church Tories digesting the implications of the idea that the abolition of Christianity might (or might not) really endanger the Church, are equally satisfying to the imagination.

It is this sort of thing from which Swift found it hard to refrain for long. To keep his comic genius from becoming universal in its irreverence, he had to run in blinkers. And even in his polished performances while he wears them, we are conscious of the destructive daimon in restraint. As the years go on the daimon becomes more savage and sombre. Whatever the cause may have been—and disappointed ambition, emotional frustration, the increasing menace of an obscure disease threatening his sanity, a profound dismay at the actual conditions in the country from which he could not escape: all these may have played their part—the universal but high-spirited irreverence of *A Tale of a Tub* does gradually pass into something more formidable: a universal nausea and disgust of humanity. Though there is plenty of fun in the first two books of *Gulliver's Travels*, by the end of the work there is precious little left of *homo sapiens* in which he may take comfort, or on which he may base a hope. The sophisticated Yahoo is perhaps the most searing vision of man that the mirror of genius has ever presented to him. Nevertheless, the fourth book of *Gulliver* is more subtle than is generally perceived, and it may be that Swift allows to humanity, in the figure of Don Pedro, the Portuguese captain who rescues Gulliver, much the same possibility of redemption that Cordelia brings to *King Lear*.

More disquieting than the ruthless moral exposure of humanity, which is the substance of *Gulliver*, and which the contemporary mind may be more willing to admit than was that of a hundred years ago, is the physical nausea of mankind which haunts the end of this great book. For one cannot escape the suspicion that Swift's deliberate degradation of man (and particularly woman) beneath the animal had a pathological origin; and this suspicion is confirmed by the nature of some of his subsequent verses. As to the causes of this evident obsession we can only speculate, but it is possible that the root of the disturbance was Swift's violent renunciation of marriage after his abortive courtship of Varina. That Swift's public career began with an effort of emotional self-repression is hardly to be doubted, and that he imposed a similar effort upon the two women who were in love with him. Nature seems to have taken a grim revenge on this naturally passionate man. To attempt to imagine the full scope of that *saeva indignatio* which tore at his heart fills one with pity, and with awe.

These are the effects of tragedy, said Aristotle; and to any sort of impartial contemplation, Swift inevitably takes on the status of a tragic hero. He is big to the imagination as no contemporary figure, in the world of letters or affairs, is big. A kind of Promethean defiance is for ever revealing itself in his attitudes, and the eagle plucks at his heart.

Yet it would be a mistake to conclude that Swift's religion was not genuine and deeply serious. It may be difficult for a modern mind to reconcile Swift's attitudes with a belief in the Christian God; but Swift's was not a modern mind. It was essentially pre-scientific; it took the existence of God for granted: and the Deism which was spreading rapidly in his day was utterly repugnant to it. Though he often spoke of religion simply as the sanction of morality, and as supplying the place of reason in the mass of humanity who were incapable of reason, we need to remember that his conception of reason was itself religious, and almost mystical. It was akin to the Platonic intuition of the Good, which conferred the power to follow it; or would do, but for the radical corruption of man's nature. Of that Swift was convinced. Thus the doctrine of original sin was compulsive to him. And to one so persuaded of the precariousness of any order whatsoever in human affairs, an overwhelming idea of the divine omnipotence—the 'all-powerful God, the least motion of whose will can create or destroy the world' is a phrase of one of his prayers—was a natural refuge. Perhaps it would be near the truth to say that his belief in the divine love took the form of a sense of the miraculous mercy of a mysterious and inscrutable God. But to suggest that it was not sincere is unwarrantable.

Swift is still a living influence in literature. The finest satire of modern times, George Orwell's *Animal Farm*, is plainly indebted both to the story of the Coat in *A Tale of a Tub*, and to the Houyhnhnms in *Gulliver*.

SWIFT

A Select Bibliography

(Place of publication London, unless stated otherwise. Detailed bibliographical information will also be found in the appropriate volume of *The Cambridge Bibliography of English Literature* and *The Oxford History of English Literature*.)

Bibliography:

A BIBLIOGRAPHY OF THE WRITINGS IN PROSE AND VERSE, by H. Teerink; The Hague (1937)
—revised edition, edited by A. H. Scouten, Philadelphia, 1963. This is a comprehensive work, superseding W. S. Jackson's Bibliography (Vol. XII of *Prose Works*, ed. T. Scott, 1908) and containing extensive lists of doubtful and supposititious writings as well as of critical and biographical studies.

CONTRIBUTIONS TOWARDS A BIBLIOGRAPHY OF 'GULLIVER'S TRAVELS', by L. L. Hubbard (1922).

THE MOTTE EDITIONS OF 'GULLIVER'S TRAVELS', by H. Williams (1925)
—see also Sir H. Williams's authoritative bibliography of the early editions in his edition of *Gulliver's Travels* (First Edition Club, 1926).

THE REPUTATION OF SWIFT, 1781-1882, by D. M. Berwick; Philadelphia (1941).

JONATHAN SWIFT: A List of Critical Studies, 1895-1945, compiled by L. A. Landa and J. E. Tobin; New York (1945)
—a valuable guide to numerous articles in learned journals, with an account of Swift MSS in American libraries, by D. H. Davis.

THE ROTHSCHILD LIBRARY, 2 vols (1954)
—contains full descriptions of the important collection of printed books, pamphlets and manuscripts by Swift formed by Lord Rothschild, with references to bibliographical studies of separate works published since Teerink.

Collected Works:

MISCELLANIES IN PROSE AND VERSE (1711)
—apart from a 16 page pamphlet (1710), the earliest collection of Swift's writings. A number of unauthorized and pirated Swiftian 'Miscellanies' of varied content were published during the following quarter of a century.

MISCELLANIES IN PROSE AND VERSE, 3 vols (1727)
—these first three volumes of the 'Swift-Pope Miscellanies' were
extended by a fourth volume ('The Third Volume') in 1732 and
a fifth in 1735. An edition in 6 volumes, containing some varia-
tions appeared in 1736. This famous collection was from the first
frequently reprinted and re-issued in various combinations of
editions and dates. By 1751 it had been extended to 13 volumes.

THE DRAPIER'S MISCELLANY; Dublin (1733)
—miscellaneous pieces in verse and prose relating to the Irish economy.

WORKS, 4 vols; Dublin (1735)
—published by Faulkner, with Swift's tacit approval, this textually
important edition was extended to 6 volumes in 1738, to 8 volumes
in 1746, to 11 volumes in 1763, and by 1769 to 20 volumes (with
the Letters). Sets of the reprinted volumes of various dates are found
in irregular combinations.

POETICAL WORKS; Dublin (1736)
— a separate reprint of Vol. II of Faulkner's second edition of the
Works. A number of separate editions of Swift's poetical works
were published during the eighteenth century and his poems were
included in the well-known series edited by Bell, Johnson, Ander-
son, Park, etc.

WORKS, ed. J. Hawkesworth, 6 or 12 vols (1755-75)
—a rival of Faulkner's edition, published simultaneously in 6 volumes
4to and 12 volumes 8vo, 1755, subsequently extended by 8 additional 4to volumes and 13 additional 8vo volumes. Also published
later in 27 volumes 18mo.

WORKS, ed. T. Sheridan, 17 vols (1784)
—based on Hawkesworth's text.

WORKS, 19 vols (1801: 24 vols (12mo) 1803)
—Sheridan's edition 'corrected and revised' by J. Nichols.

WORKS, ed. Sir W. Scott, 19 vols; Edinburgh (1814: 2nd ed. 1824;
reprinted 1883)
—Vol. I contains Scott's long biographical essay.

PROSE WORKS, ed, T. Scott, 12 vols (1897-1908)
—Vol XII is a Bibliography by W. S. Jackson.

THE DRAPIER'S LETTERS TO THE PEOPLE OF IRELAND AGAINST RECEIVING
WOOD'S HALFPENCE, ed. H. Davis; Oxford (1935)
—the definitive edition.

PROSE WORKS, ed. H. Davis, 15 vols; Oxford (1939-64)
—the definitive 'Shakespeare Head' edition, with valuable introductions and bibliographical and textual notes.

POEMS, ed. H. Williams, 3 vols; Oxford (1937)
—the definitive edition; second edition, revised, 1958.

COLLECTED POEMS, ed. J. Horrell, 2 vols (1958)
—in the Muses' Library.

Selected Works:

Among the many selections from Swift's writings, ranging from school texts to limited editions-de-luxe and including volumes in such series as Everyman's Library, Collin's Classics etc., the following are noteworthy: *Satires and Personal Writings* (ed. W. A. Eddy), 1932; *Gulliver's Travels and Selected Prose and Verse* (Nonesuch Press, ed. J. Hayward), 1934; *Selected Prose Works* (Cresset Library, ed. J. Hayward), 1949.

Letters:

LETTERS TO AND FROM DR J. SWIFT, 1714-1738; Dublin (1741)
—also published as Vol. VII of Faulkner's edition of *Works*.

LETTERS, ed. J. Hawkesworth (1766).

LETTERS, ed. J. Hawkesworth and D. Swift, 6 vols (1768-9)
—published as part of Hawkesworth's edition of *Works*.

UNPUBLISHED LETTERS, ed. G. B. Hill (1899).

VANESSA AND HER CORRESPONDENCE WITH SWIFT, ed. A. M. Freeman (1921)
—the first publication of the 'love letters' of Swift and Esther Vanhomrigh.

LETTERS TO CHARLES FORD, ed. D. Nichol Smith; Oxford (1935)
—edited for the first time from the originals, now for the most part in the Rothschild Library.

THE JOURNAL TO STELLA, ed. H. Williams, 2 vols; Oxford (1948)
—the definitive edition. The letters to Esther Johnson, comprising the so-called 'Journal to Stella', were first printed, more or less inaccurately, in Hawkesworth's *Works*, Vol. X, 1766 (Letters 1 and 41-65) and in Vol. XII, 1768 (Letters 2-40). Later editions: ed. G. A. Aitken, 1901; ed. F. Ryland (Vol. II of T. Scott's edition of *Works*, 1905); ed. J. K. Moorhead, 1924 (Everyman's Library).

Separate Works:

Note: This section does not include single pieces printed as broadsides
or as folio half-sheets; contributions to periodicals (e.g. *The Tatler,
The Examiner*), and to books by other writers, for which see *Prose
Works*, ed. H. Davis, and *Poems*, ed. H. Williams; or any of the
numerous doubtful or supposititious works which at various times
have been ascribed to Swift. (For the titles of the latter, see Teerink's
Bibliography and the excellent short-title list by H. Williams in
CBEL)

A DISCOURSE OF THE CONTESTS AND DISSENSIONS BETWEEN THE NOBLES
    AND THE COMMONS IN ATHENS AND ROME (1701). *Politics*

A TALE OF A TUB [AND THE BATTLE OF THE BOOKS] (1704). *Polemical
    Satire*

—annotated edition, with plates, 1710. *The Batttle of the Books* was
    Swift's contribution to the famous Quarrel of the Ancients and the
    Moderns. The definitive edition of both works was edited by
    A. Guthkelch and D. Nichol Smith, Oxford, 1920.

PREDICTIONS FOR THE YEAR 1708 (1708). *Parody*

—the first of several jesting satires against almanac-makers (and
    one, Partridge, in particular), written under the pseudonym of
    Isaac Bickerstaff during 1708-9.

A PROJECT FOR THE ADVANCEMENT OF RELIGION AND THE REFORMATION
    OF MANNERS (1709). *Moral Instruction*

A LETTER . . . CONCERNING THE SACRAMENTAL TEST (1709). *Church
    Politics*

BAUCIS AND PHILEMON (1709). *Verse*

—Swift's first separately printed poem. Reprinted with other poems
    and with the prose parody, *A Meditation upon a Broom-Stick*, in
    1710.

THE EXAMINER. (1710-11). *Political Journalism*

—32 weekly issues, beginning with No. 14, 26 Oct 1710, were written
    by Swift.

A SHORT CHARACTER OF . . . [THE EARL OF WHARTON] (1711). *Invective*

SOME REMARKS UPON A PAMPHLET (1711). *Politics*

A NEW JOURNEY TO PARIS (1711). *Politics*

A LEARNED COMMENT UPON DR HARE'S EXCELLENT SERMON (1711).
    Church Politics

THE CONDUCT OF THE ALLIES (1712[1711]). *Politics*

—the definitive edition was edited, with introduction and notes, by
    C. B. Wheeler, Oxford, 1916.

SOME ADVICE HUMBLY OFFER'D TO THE MEMBERS OF THE OCTOBER CLUB (1712). *Politics*

SOME REMARKS ON THE BARRIER TREATY (1712). *Politics*

A PROPOSAL FOR CORRECTING . . . THE ENGLISH TONGUE (1712). *Criticism*

SOME REASONS TO PROVE THAT NO PERSON IS OBLIGED BY HIS PRINCIPLES AS A WHIG, ETC. (1712). *Politics*

A LETTER OF THANKS . . . TO THE . . . BISHOP OF S. ASAPH (1712). *Church Politics*

MR. C[OLLI]N'S DISCOURSE OF FREE-THINKING (1713). *Polemics*

PART OF THE SEVENTH EPISTLE OF THE FIRST BOOK OF HORACE IMITATED (1713). *Verse*

THE IMPORTANCE OF THE GUARDIAN CONSIDERED (1713). *Politics*

THE FIRST ODE OF THE SECOND BOOK OF HORACE PARAPHRAS'D (171[4]). *Verse*

THE PUBLICK SPIRIT OF THE WHIGS (1714). *Politics*

AN ARGUMENT TO PROVE THAT THE ABOLISHING OF CHRISTIANITY IN ENGLAND, ETC. (1717)
—first published in the *Miscellanies*, 1711.

A PROPOSAL FOR THE UNIVERSAL USE OF IRISH MANUFACTURE (1720). *Political Economy*
—*A Defence of English Commodities*, 1720, an answer to this pamphlet, was probably written by Swift.

A LETTER . . . TO A GENTLEMAN DESIGNING FOR HOLY ORDERS (1720). *Criticism*

THE SWEARER'S BANK (1720). *Satire*

THE BUBBLE (1721). *Verse*

A LETTER OF ADVICE TO A YOUNG POET; Dublin (1721). *Criticism*
—long ascribed to Swift but probably not by him.

SOME ARGUMENTS AGAINST ENLARGING THE POWER OF THE BISHOPS (1723). *Church Politics*

A LETTER TO THE SHOP-KEEPERS (1724). *Political Economy*
—the first of the celebrated 'Drapier's Letters.'

A LETTER TO MR HARDING THE PRINTER (1724). *Political Economy*
—the second of the 'Drapier's Letters'.

SOME OBSERVATIONS UPON A PAPER (1724). *Political Economy*
—the third of the 'Drapier's Letters'.

A LETTER TO THE WHOLE PEOPLE OF IRELAND (1724). *Political Economy*
—the fourth of the 'Drapier's Letters'.

A LETTER TO . . . VISCOUNT MOLESWORTH (1724). *Political Economy*
—the fifth and last of the 'Drapier's Letters'. They were published together in Dublin in 1725 as *Fraud Detected: or, the Hibernian Patriot*. The definitive edition of the *Drapier's Letters* was edited by H. Davis; Oxford, 1935.

THE BIRTH OF MANLY VIRTUE (1725). *Verse*

CADENUS AND VANESSA: A Poem (1726). *Verse*

[GULLIVER'S] TRAVELS INTO SEVERAL REMOTE NATIONS OF THE WORLD, 2 vols (1726). *Satirical Fantasy*
—Faulkner's text (*Works*, 1735, Vol. III), which was revised with Swift's co-operation, was first reprinted in modern times in the 'Nonesuch' *Swift*, and later in the Cresset Library *Swift*, in the 'Shakespeare Head' *Swift* (Vol. XI), and in Collin's Classics. The definitive edition of the text of the first edition of 1726 was elaborately edited by H. Williams for the First Edition Club in 1926.

A SHORT VIEW OF THE STATE OF IRELAND; Dublin (1727-8). *Political Economy*

AN ANSWER TO A PAPER CALLED 'A MEMORIAL OF THE POOR INHABITANTS'; Dublin (1728). *Political Economy*

THE INTELLIGENCER; Dublin (1728). *Political Journalism*
—20 weekly numbers by Swift and Sheridan. Published as a volume in 1729. No. 19 was printed separately in 1736 as *A Letter . . . to a Country Gentleman in the North of Ireland*.

A MODEST PROPOSAL; Dublin 1729). *Sociological Satire*

THE JOURNAL OF A DUBLIN LADY; Dublin (1729). *Verse*
—reprinted in London as *The Journal of a Modern Lady*.

A PANEGYRIC ON . . . DEAN SWIFT; Dublin (1729-30). *Verse*

AN EPISTLE TO . . . LORD CARTERET; Dublin (1730). *Politics*

AN EPISTLE UPON AN EPISTLE; Dublin (1730). *Verse*

A LIBEL ON D[OCTOR] D[ELANY] (1730). *Verse*

A VINDICATION OF . . . LORD CARTERET (1730). *Politics*

TRAULUS [Two parts, Dublin] (1730). *Verse*

HORACE, BOOK I: ODE XIV [Dublin] ([17]30). *Verse*

A SOLDIER AND A SCHOLAR (1732). *Verse*
—reprinted (Dublin, 1732) as *The Grand Question Debated*.

CONSIDERATIONS UPON TWO BILLS (1732). *Church Politics*

AN EXAMINATION OF CERTAIN ABUSES; Dublin (1732). *Sociological Satire*
—the title of the London edition (1732) begins: *City Cries, Instrumental and Vocal*.

THE LADY'S DRESSING ROOM (1732). *Verse*

THE ADVANTAGES PROPOSED BY REPEALING THE SACRAMENTAL TEST; Dublin (1732). *Church Politics*

AN ELEGY ON DICKY AND DOLLY; Dublin (1732). *Verse*

THE LIFE AND GENUINE CHARACTER OF DOCTOR SWIFT. WRITTEN BY HIMSELF (1733). *Verse*

ON POETRY: A Rapsody (1733). *Verse*

THE PRESBYTERIANS' PLEA OF MERIT; Dublin (1733). *Church Politics*

SOME REASONS AGAINST THE BILL FOR SETTLING THE TYTH OF HEMP BY A MODUS; Dublin (1734). *Political Economy*

AN EPISTLE TO A LADY . . . ALSO A POEM . . . CALLED THE UNIVERSAL PASSION (1734). *Verse*

A BEAUTIFUL YOUNG NYMPH GOING TO BED (1734). *Verse*
—also contains 'Strephon and Chloe' and 'Cassinus and Peter'.

A PROPOSAL FOR GIVING BADGES TO THE BEGGARS . . . OF DUBLIN; Dublin (1737). *Sociology*

AN IMITATION OF THE SIXTH SATIRE OF THE SECOND BOOK OF HORACE (1738). *Verse*
—written in 1714 and completed by Pope.

THE BEASTS' CONFESSION TO THE PRIEST; Dublin (1738). *Verse*

A COMPLETE COLLECTION OF GENTEEL AND INGENIOUS CONVERSATION (1738). *Social Satire*
—published under the pseudonym of Simon Wagstaff.

VERSES ON THE DEATH OF DR SWIFT. WRITTEN BY HIMSELF (1739). *Verse*
—incorporates part of *The Life and Genuine Character* (1733). The text of the 4 folio editions of 1739, published by Bathurst in London, is inferior to the text of the 6 octavo editions published in Dublin by Faulkner in the same year.

SOME FREE THOUGHTS UPON THE PRESENT STATE OF AFFAIRS; Dublin (1741). *Politics*

THREE SERMONS (1744). *Theology*
—a fourth sermon was added to the second edition of the same year.

DIRECTIONS TO SERVANTS; Dublin (1745). *Social Satire*

BROTHERLY LOVE: A Sermon; Dublin (1754). *Theology*

THE HISTORY OF THE FOUR LAST YEARS OF THE QUEEN (1758). *History*

Biography and Criticism:

MEMOIRS [OF LAETITIA PILKINGTON], 3 vols (1748-54)
—lively but somewhat fanciful first-hand reminiscences.

REMARKS ON THE LIFE AND WRITINGS OF JONATHAN SWIFT, by John, Earl of Orrery (1752)
—see also P. Delany's more important *Observations on Lord Orrery's Remarks*, 1754.

LIFE OF DR SWIFT, by J. Hawkesworth; Dublin (1755)
—first printed in Vol. I of Hawkesworth's edition of Swift's *Works*.

AN ESSAY UPON THE LIFE, WRITINGS AND CHARACTER OF DR JONATHAN SWIFT, by D. Swift (1755)
—by Swift's cousin, Deane Swift.

LIFE, by W. H. Dilworth (1758).

LIFE, by S. Johnson [in *Lives of the Poets*, Vol. III] (1781).

LIFE, by T. Sheridan (1784).

ESSAY ON THE EARLIER PART OF THE LIFE OF SWIFT, by J. Barrett (1808).

MEMOIRS OF JONATHAN SWIFT, by Sir W. Scott, 2 vols; Paris (1826)
—first printed in Vol. I of Scott's edition of *Works*, 1814.

THE CLOSING YEARS OF DEAN SWIFT'S LIFE, by Sir W. Wilde (1849).

THE ENGLISH HUMOURISTS OF THE 18TH CENTURY, by W. M. Thackeray (1851)
—contains a famous essay on Swift.

JONATHAN SWIFT: Sa vie et ses œuvres, by L. Prevost-Paradol; Paris (1856).

LIFE, by J. Forster (1875)
—only Vol. I was published. The Forster Collection in the Library of the Victoria and Albert Museum, London, contains important manuscript and printed material by and relating to Swift.

SWIFT, by L. Stephen (1882)
—in the 'English Men of Letters' series.

LIFE, by H. Craik (1882: 2 vols, 1894).

JONATHAN SWIFT: A Biographical and Critical Study, by J. C. Collins (1893).

DEAN SWIFT AND HIS WRITINGS, by G. P. Moriarty (1893).

SWIFT IN IRELAND, by R. A. King (1895).

THE ORRERY PAPERS, 2 vols (1903).

SWIFT, by C. Whibley (1917)
—the Leslie Stephen lecture, 1917.

GULLIVER'S TRAVELS: A Critical Study, by W. A. Eddy; Princeton (1923).

SWIFT EN FRANCE, by S. Goulding; Paris (1924).

SWIFT: Les années de jeunesse et 'Le Conte du Tonneau', by E. Pons; Strasbourg (1925)
—the first instalment of a massive but uncompleted critical biography.

SWIFT'S VERSE, by F. E. Ball (1928).

THE SKULL OF SWIFT, by S. Leslie (1928).

DO WHAT YOU WILL, by A. Huxley (1929)
—contains an essay on Swift.

SWIFT, by C. Van Doren (1931).

DEAN SWIFT'S LIBRARY, by H. Williams (1932)
—contains a facsimile of the catalogue of Swift's Library.

THE LIFE AND FRIENDSHIPS OF DEAN SWIFT, by S. Gwynn (1933)
—a popular biography.

JONATHAN SWIFT: A Critical Essay, by W. D. Taylor (1933).

THE SCRIPT OF JONATHAN SWIFT AND OTHER ESSAYS, by S. Leslie; Philadelphia (1935).

LA PENSÉE RELIGIEUSE DE SWIFT ET SES ANTINOMIES, by C. Looten; Lille (1935).

THE MIND AND ART OF JONATHAN SWIFT, by R. Quintana (1936)
—an important critical study. Revised edition, 1953.

SWIFT'S MARRIAGE TO STELLA, by M.B. Gold; Cambridge, Mass. (1937)
—a careful analysis of all the available evidence relating to this vexed problem.

JONATHAN SWIFT, by B. Newman (1937).

FROM ANNE TO VICTORIA, edited by B. Dobrée (1937)
—valuable essay on Swift by J. Hayward.

JONATHAN SWIFT, DEAN AND PASTOR, by R. W. Jackson (1939).

STELLA, by H. Davis; New York (1942).

SWIFT AND HIS CIRCLE, by R. W. Jackson; Dublin (1945).

JONATHAN SWIFT: A List of critical studies published from 1895 to 1945, by L. A. Landa and J. E. Tobin; New York (1945).

FOUR ESSAYS ON 'GULLIVER'S TRAVELS', by A.E. Case; Princeton (1945)
—defends the 1726 text against Faulkner's revised text of 1735.

THE SATIRE OF JONATHAN SWIFT, by H. Davis; New York (1947).

SHOOTING AN ELEPHANT, by G. Orwell (1950)
—includes an essay on Gulliver.

SWIFT'S SATIRE ON LEARNING IN 'A TALE OF A TUB', by M.K. Starkman; Princeton (1952).

THE COMMON PURSUIT, by F. R. Leavis (1952)
—contains an important study, entitled 'Swift's Irony'.
THE TEXT OF 'GULLIVER'S TRAVELS', by H. Williams (1953)
—the Sanders Lectures, 1953. A defence of Faulkner's text of 1735.
JONATHAN SWIFT AND THE ANATOMY OF SATIRE: A Study of Satirical
   Technique, by J. M. Bullitt; Harvard (1953).
JONATHAN SWIFT: A Critical Biography, by J. M. Murry (1954).
THE MASKS OF JONATHAN SWIFT, by W. M. Ewald jr. (1954)
—a study of the *personae* adopted by Swift.
SWIFT AND THE CHURCH OF IRELAND, by L. A. Landa (1954)
—an important piece of research.
SWIFT: An Introduction, by R. Quintana; Oxford (1955)
—paperback edition, 1962. A masterly condensation.
SWIFT AND CARROLL, by P. Greenacre; New York (1955)
—a psychological study according to Freudian principles.
THE PEN AND THE SWORD, by M. M. Foot (1957).
THE PERSONALITY OF JONATHAN SWIFT, by I. Ehrenpreis (1958).
IN SEARCH OF SWIFT, by D. Johnston; Dublin (1959).
JONATHAN SWIFT AND THE AGE OF COMPROMISE, by K. Williams (1959).
DEAN SWIFT, by D. F. R. Wilson; Dublin [1960].
SWIFT'S CLASSICAL RHETORIC, by C. A. Beaumont; Athens, Georgia
   (1961).
THE CURSE OF PARTY: Swift's relations with Addison and Steele, by
   B. A. Goldgar; Lincoln, Nebraska (1961).
JONATHAN SWIFT AND IRELAND, by O.W. Ferguson; Urbana (1962).
SAMUEL BECKETT ET JONATHAN SWIFT: Vers une étude comparée,
   by J. Fletcher; Toulouse (1962).
CADENUS: A Reassessment . . . of the relationship between Swift,
   Stella and Vanessa, by S. le Brocquy; Dublin (1962).
JONATHAN SWIFT: De Engelse Voltaire, by J. L. Snethlage; The
   Hague (1962).
JONATHAN SWIFT, by N. S. Subramanyam; Allahabad (1962).
SWIFT: The Man, his Works and the Age, by I. Ehrenpreis, Vol I,
   MR SWIFT AND HIS CONTEMPORARIES (1962).
REASON AND IMAGINATION, ed. J. A. Mazzeo (1962)
—contains an essay by R.S. Crane on Book IV of *Gulliver's Travels*.
SWIFT AND THE SATIRIST'S ART, by E. W. Rosenheim (1963).
JONATHAN SWIFT, by H. Davis; New York (1964)
—contains essays on Swift's Satire and other studies.

JONATHAN SWIFT: Essays on his satire and other studies, by H. J. Davis (1964).

JONATHAN SWIFT: A short character, by N. Dennis (New York 1964, London, 1965).

SWIFT, LE VÉRITABLE GULLIVER, by P. Frédérix; Paris (1964).

SWIFT: A Collection of critical essays, by E. Tuveson; Englewood Cliffs (1964).

SWIFT AND THE TWENTIETH CENTURY, by M. Voigt; Detroit (1964).

SWIFT'S USE OF THE BIBLE: A Documentation and study in allusion, by C. A. Beaumont; Athens, Georgia (1965).

THE USES OF IRONY: Papers on Defoe and Swift, by M. E. Novak; Los Angeles, (1966).

—includes 'Swift's Use of Irony' by H. T. Davis,

JONATHAN SWIFT: Romantic and cynic moralist, by J. G. Gilbert (1966).

JONATHAN SWIFT 1667-1967: A Dublin tercentenary tribute, ed. R. J. MacHugh and P. W. Edwards; Dublin (1967).

SWIFT, by P. Wolff-Windegg; Stuttgart (1967).

A QUANTITATIVE APPROACH TO THE STYLE OF JONATHAN SWIFT, by L. T. Milic; The Hague (1967).

JONATHAN SWIFT AS A TORY PAMPHLETEER, by R. I. Cook (1967).

SWIFT: Modern judgements, ed. A. N. Jeffares (1968).

THE WORLD OF JONATHAN SWIFT: Essays for the tercentenary, collected and ed. B. Vickers; Oxford (1968).

JONATHAN SWIFT, by K. Williams (1968).

JONATHAN SWIFT: A critical introduction, by D. Donoghue (1969).

SWIFT, by W. A. Speck (1969).

SWIFT: The critical heritage, ed. K. Williams (1970).

WRITERS AND THEIR WORK

General Surveys:

THE DETECTIVE STORY IN BRITAIN:
Julian Symons
THE ENGLISH BIBLE: Donald Coggan
ENGLISH VERSE EPIGRAM:
G. Rostrevor Hamilton
ENGLISH HYMNS: A. Pollard
ENGLISH MARITIME WRITING:
Hakluyt to Cook: Oliver Warner
THE ENGLISH SHORT STORY I: & II:
T. O. Beachcroft
THE ENGLISH SONNET: P. Cruttwell
ENGLISH SERMONS: Arthur Pollard
ENGLISH TRAVELLERS IN THE
NEAR EAST: Robin Fedden
THREE WOMEN DIARISTS: M. Willy

Sixteenth Century and Earlier:

FRANCIS BACON: J. Max Patrick
BEAUMONT & FLETCHER: Ian Fletcher
CHAUCER: Nevill Coghill
GOWER & LYDGATE: Derek Pearsall
RICHARD HOOKER: A. Pollard
THOMAS KYD: Philip Edwards
LANGLAND: Nevill Coghill
LYLY & PEELE: G. K. Hunter
MALORY: M. C. Bradbrook
MARLOWE: Philip Henderson
SIR THOMAS MORE: E. E. Reynolds
RALEGH: Agnes Latham
SIDNEY: Kenneth Muir
SKELTON: Peter Green
SPENSER: Rosemary Freeman
THREE 14TH-CENTURY ENGLISH
MYSTICS: Phyllis Hodgson
TWO SCOTS CHAUCERIANS:
H. Harvey Wood
WYATT: Sergio Baldi

Seventeenth Century:

SIR THOMAS BROWNE: Peter Green
BUNYAN: Henri Talon
CAVALIER POETS: Robin Skelton
CONGREVE: Bonamy Dobrée
DONNE: F. Kermode
DRYDEN: Bonamy Dobrée
ENGLISH DIARISTS:
Evelyn and Pepys: M. Willy
FARQUHAR: A. J. Farmer
JOHN FORD: Clifford Leech
GEORGE HERBERT: T. S. Eliot
HERRICK: John Press
HOBBES: T. E. Jessop
BEN JONSON: J. B. Bamborough
LOCKE: Maurice Cranston
ANDREW MARVELL: John Press
MILTON: E. M. W. Tillyard

RESTORATION COURT POETS:
V. de S. Pinto
SHAKESPEARE: C. J. Sisson
CHRONICLES: Clifford Leech
EARLY COMEDIES: Derek Traversi
LATER COMEDIES: G. K. Hunter
FINAL PLAYS: F. Kermode
HISTORIES: L. C. Knights
POEMS: F. T. Prince
PROBLEM PLAYS: Peter Ure
ROMAN PLAYS: T. J. B. Spencer
GREAT TRAGEDIES: Kenneth Muir
THREE METAPHYSICAL POETS:
Margaret Willy
IZAAK WALTON: Margaret Bottrall
WEBSTER: Ian Scott-Kilvert
WYCHERLEY: P. F. Vernon

Eighteenth Century:

BERKELEY: T. E. Jessop
BLAKE: Kathleen Raine
BOSWELL: P. A. W. Collins
BURKE: T. E. Utley
BURNS: David Daiches
WM. COLLINS: Oswald Doughty
COWPER: N. Nicholson
CRABBE: R. L. Brett
DEFOE: J. R. Sutherland
FIELDING: John Butt
GAY: Oliver Warner
GIBBON: C. V. Wedgwood
GOLDSMITH: A. Norman Jeffares
GRAY: R. W. Ketton-Cremer
HUME: Montgomery Belgion
JOHNSON: S. C. Roberts
POPE: Ian Jack
RICHARDSON: R. F. Brissenden
SHERIDAN: W. A. Darlington
CHRISTOPHER SMART: G. Grigson
SMOLLETT: Laurence Brander
STEELE, ADDISON: A. R. Humphreys
STERNE: D. W. Jefferson
SWIFT: J. Middleton Murry
SIR JOHN VANBRUGH: Bernard Harris
HORACE WALPOLE: Hugh Honour

Nineteenth Century:

MATTHEW ARNOLD: Kenneth Allott
JANE AUSTEN: S. Townsend Warner
BAGEHOT: N. St John-Stevas
THE BRONTË SISTERS: P. Bentley
BROWNING: John Bryson
E. B. BROWNING: Alethea Hayter
SAMUEL BUTLER: G. D. H. Cole
BYRON: Bernard Blackstone
CARLYLE: David Gascoyne
LEWIS CARROLL: Derek Hudson
CLOUGH: Isobel Armstrong

COLERIDGE: Kathleen Raine
CREEVEY & GREVILLE: J. Richardson
DE QUINCEY: Hugh Sykes Davies
DICKENS: K. J. Fielding
　EARLY NOVELS: T. Blount
　LATER NOVELS: B. Hardy
DISRAELI: Paul Bloomfield
GEORGE ELIOT: Lettice Cooper
FERRIER & GALT: W. M. Parker
FITZGERALD: Joanna Richardson
MRS. GASKELL: Miriam Allott
GISSING: A. C. Ward
THOMAS HARDY: R. A. Scott-James
　　　　　　　and C. Day Lewis
HAZLITT: J. B. Priestley
HOOD: Laurence Brander
G. M. HOPKINS: Geoffrey Grigson
T. H. HUXLEY: William Irvine
KEATS: Edmund Blunden
LAMB: Edmund Blunden
LANDOR: G. Rostrevor Hamilton
EDWARD LEAR: Joanna Richardson
MACAULAY: G. R. Potter
MEREDITH: Phyllis Bartlett
JOHN STUART MILL: M. Cranston
WILLIAM MORRIS: P. Henderson
NEWMAN: J. M. Cameron
PATER: Iain Fletcher
PEACOCK: J. I. M. Stewart
ROSSETTI: Oswald Doughty
CHRISTINA ROSSETTI: G. Battiscombe
RUSKIN: Peter Quennell
SIR WALTER SCOTT: Ian Jack
SHELLEY: G. M. Matthews
SOUTHEY: Geoffrey Carnall
R. L. STEVENSON: G. B. Stern
SWINBURNE: H. J. C. Grierson
TENNYSON: F. L. Lucas
THACKERAY: Laurence Brander
FRANCIS THOMPSON: P. Butter
TROLLOPE: Hugh Sykes Davies
OSCAR WILDE: James Laver
WORDSWORTH: Helen Darbishire

Twentieth Century:
CHINUA ACHEBE: A. Ravenscroft
W. H. AUDEN: Richard Hoggart
HILAIRE BELLOC: Renée Haynes
ARNOLD BENNETT: F. Swinnerton
EDMUND BLUNDEN: Alec M. Hardie
ELIZABETH BOWEN: Jocelyn Brooke
ROBERT BRIDGES: J. Sparrow
ROY CAMPBELL: David Wright
JOYCE CARY: Walter Allen
G. K. CHESTERTON: C. Hollis
WINSTON CHURCHILL: John Connell
R. G. COLLINGWOOD: E.W.F. Tomlin
I. COMPTON-BURNETT: P. H. Johnson
JOSEPH CONRAD: Oliver Warner

WALTER DE LA MARE: K. Hopkins
NORMAN DOUGLAS: Ian Greenlees
LAWRENCE DURRELL: G. S. Fraser
T. S. ELIOT: M. C. Bradbrook
FIRBANK & BETJEMAN: J. Brooke
FORD MADOX FORD: Kenneth Young
E. M. FORSTER: Rex Warner
CHRISTOPHER FRY: Derek Stanford
JOHN GALSWORTHY: R. H. Mottram
WM. GOLDING: Clive Pemberton
ROBERT GRAVES: M. Seymour-Smith
GRAHAM GREENE: Francis Wyndham
L. P. HARTLEY & ANTHONY POWELL:
　　　　P. Bloomfield and B. Bergonzi
A. E. HOUSMAN: Ian Scott-Kilvert
ALDOUS HUXLEY: Jocelyn Brooke
HENRY JAMES: Michael Swan
PAMELA HANSFORD JOHNSON:
　　　　　　　　　Isabel Quigly
JAMES JOYCE: J. I. M. Stewart
RUDYARD KIPLING: Bonamy Dobrée
D. H. LAWRENCE: Kenneth Young
C. DAY LEWIS: Clifford Dyment
WYNDHAM LEWIS: E. W. F. Tomlin
COMPTON MACKENZIE: K. Young
LOUIS MACNEICE: John Press
KATHERINE MANSFIELD: Ian Gordon
JOHN MASEFIELD: L. A. G. Strong
SOMERSET MAUGHAM: J. Brophy
GEORGE MOORE: A. Norman Jeffares
EDWIN MUIR: J. C. Hall
J. MIDDLETON MURRY: Philip Mairet
SEAN O'CASEY: W. A. Armstrong
GEORGE ORWELL: Tom Hopkinson
POETS OF 1939-45 WAR: R. N. Currey
POWYS BROTHERS: R. C. Churchill
J. B. PRIESTLEY: Ivor Brown
HERBERT READ: Francis Berry
FOUR REALIST NOVELISTS: V. Brome
BERNARD SHAW: A. C. Ward
EDITH SITWELL: John Lehmann
OSBERT SITWELL: Roger Fulford
KENNETH SLESSOR: C. Semmler
C. P. SNOW: William Cooper
STRACHEY: R. A. Scott-James
SYNGE & LADY GREGORY: E. Coxhead
DYLAN THOMAS: G. S. Fraser
EDWARD THOMAS: Vernon Scannell
G. M. TREVELYAN: J. H. Plumb
WAR POETS: 1914-18: E. Blunden
EVELYN WAUGH: Christopher Hollis
H. G. WELLS: Montgomery Belgion
PATRICK WHITE: R. F. Brissenden
CHARLES WILLIAMS: J. Heath-Stubbs
ANGUS WILSON: K. W. Gransden
VIRGINIA WOOLF: B. Blackstone
W. B. YEATS: G. S. Fraser
ANDREW YOUNG & R. S. THOMAS:
　　　　　L. Clark and R. G. Thomas